T0064100

Twiddling Thumbs

Kesh Kumar

AuthorHouse™
1663 Liberty Drive
Bloomington, IN 47403
www.authorhouse.com
Phone: 1-800-839-8640

Published by AuthorHouse 11/14/2014

ISBN: 978-1-4969-1606-8 (sc)

DEDICATION

When the denerian became a vicenarian,

the familial pioneer became provincial.

By the time he became a septuagenarian,

the provincial pioneer,

had become international.

Phenomenal accomplishment!

This book is dedicated to:

- A stellar septuagenarian.

  A magnanimous man, an inspiration.

  Umar Persaud Sharma.

  AND

- **Purawatty** *aka* **Loretta /Lalita**, his spouse and steadfast supporter.

- **Endira** and **Ghajindra Sharma**: the dazzling dawn and spectacular

  sunset that enrich his days.

ACKNOWLEDGMENT

"I am who I am because of who we all are."

The compilation and publication of this collection has been inspired by the delightful spirit of camaraderie that hovers over the Ubuntu Village at TAIBU.

On observing the unreserved pride Kareen Marshall showed when displaying a copy of *Caught in the Maelstrom. Teenage Dilemma*, an onlooker could have easily assumed that it was her creation. My book was her book; my joy was hers; my success was hers and vice versa. Her action exemplified the spirit of the Ubuntu Village and the meaning of the motto: "I am who I am because of who we all are."

And the senior villagers Liben and Tony readily joined in the celebrations, playing the djembe, dancing to the beat, thereby providing the impetus for the publication of *Twiddling Thumbs*.

My sincerest gratitude to these three stellar village leaders at TAIBU:

Liben Gebremikael.

Tony Jno Baptiste.

Kareen Marshall.

CONTENTS

TWIDDLING THUMBS

If I twiddle my right thumb,
make sure you say yes.
If I twiddle my left,
be sure you say no.
If I don't twiddle at all,
say you do not know,
or cannot recall.
The twiddling and answering
went well for a while.
but after the adjournment,
things really went awry.
The lawyer twiddled his right thumb,
the client said no.
The lawyer twiddled his left thumb,
the client said yes.
The lawyer grew outraged,
and stopped all the twiddling.
The client grew confused,
and remained dead silent.
The judge grew impatient,
and rebuked the client.
The client grew flustered,
and yelled at the lawyer:
It's your bloody fault,
for twiddling right thumb and left,
at the same god damned time.
Did you want me to answer
yes and no to the same question?
Do you think I am a lawyer, too?

AWAKING DEAD

With big, bald, head,
melding forehead,
and bulging blue eyes,
that danced excitedly,
he was an affable man
with cheerful demeanour,
and a manic passion
for appeasing his stomach.
He had a soup bowl the size
of Mambrino's helmet,
and a personalised knife
to carve chops and steak.
The contentment in his eyes,
his ever present smile,
gave ample evidence
of deepest euphoria.
Once he told someone,
whose curious eyes he caught
that he'd have no regret,
if one day he woke dead,
for he, without a doubt,
should have had his fill.

Besides, his fulsome spouse,
a lawyer of great repute,
would sue the restaurateurs,
for enticing him to eat,
till at last he woke up dead.

EXPATRIATE CLIENT

An elderly judge retired,
another withdrew from the case
the third suffered a head stroke,
the fourth had a heart attack,
the fifth contracted flatulence,
and was fired from the bench.

All these events occurred,
while the dad led the law firm.
When he died of tongue cancer,
his older son took over.
and reopened the old files
about two or three years later.

A few more judges died,
or retired from the bench,
so the deed had not been passed
when the expatriate client,
remigrated to her country
to enjoy her endowment

The lawyer went on vacation.
But the client bided her time.
She tried to confront him.
He went into hiding.
She found out, not long after,
that the lawyer was inflicted,
with the dreaded disease,
and was covered all over

with oozing lesions.
He had grown so despondent,
he took his gun, one day
and blew up his brain to bits.

Both your dad and granddad died
of the dreaded disease,
so you be careful, now,
said the expatriate client
to the lawyer's son,
the new leader
of the old law firm.

AJAA'S DIET

My ajaa sat like a yogi:
back bolt upright,
both legs crossed.
It was an exacting posture,
I learnt when I grew older,
and tried to practice yoga,
for all my bones ached
and my whole body balked.
Ajaa closed his eyes and prayed,
ate satwaa for breakfast
and drank herbal tea;
I eat bacon on the run,
and gulp coffee double double.

Ajaa ate dhal and roti,
and rice and curried veggies.
He stayed strong and healthy,
till he died in his nineties.
I eat pork chops and pot roast
and potatoes slathered with gravy.
By the time I was forty,
I was taking medication
for high cholesterol
and hypertension.
My ajaa was deemed eccentric
because he came from India,
where he acquired the habit
of eating *weird, unwholesome* food.
When he died old age
he fit neatly in his casket
which six men bore with ease.
I guess with me it will be different.
They'll have to eviscerate me,
and build an oversized box.
to accommodate my corpse.

CURRY

This curry is delicious!
He licks his lips and burps,
as he savours hot dhal.

This curry is awesome!
He affirms, enjoying
a bowl of sweet korma
with chunks of ripe mango.

This curry is stupendous
with rice or chapatti,
the patron exclaimed,
as he ate fried potato
and eggplant, one afternoon.

Sensational, he cried,
spooning hot chili peppers
into his ravenous mouth.
Then wheezing and squeezing
he dashed for the john
and never came back
to eat curry again.

EATING

His blue eyes gleamed,
like the diamond studs
in his right ear and left.
His pharynx bobbed wildly
as he packed in beef wellington
and baked potatoes with sour cream.
He ripped open a roll,
spread layers of butter.
Beef wellington, baked potatoes,
salad submerged with dressing.
He crammed his craw continually,
like the big honey blonde,
at the Wing Machine at King,
who thrust her head forward,
clutched wings in both hands,
and nibbled and gnawed,
right down to the bare bones,
only pausing to gulp
from her jug of pale ale.

The guzzling of beef wellington
was fitting subject matter
for study in epicurean eating.
But the frenzied activity
of the blonde eating chicken wings,
gave rise to grave misgiving.
What if the hungry woman
had swallowed a few bones,
without taking notice,
and those same bones got stuck,
diagonally in her pharynx
or worse, yet, in her anus
when she went to the john?
Won't that be disastrous!

HOT

Hot! Hot! Hot!
I like my pepper pot hot,
I like my pea-soup hot,
I like my pilaf hot,
I like my cook-up hot.

Hot! Hot! Hot!
I like my okra hot,
I like my ackee hot,
I like my dumpling hot,
I like my plantain hot.

Hot! Hot! Hot!
I like my cod fish hot,
I like my coo coo hot,
I like my meat balls hot.
I like my metagee hot.

Hot! Hot! Hot!
I like them hot, hot hot!

No! my stomach
isn't lined with leather, brother
is yours lined with lesions?

LUNCH BOX

As he had been doing
everyday, for many years,
Ram removed the note
taped atop his lunch box,
and read breathlessly:
"I love you more today,
a whole bunch more, dear,
than yesterday and the day before.
Have a good lunch!"

"Thank you, my dear," Ram wrote,
at the foot of the note,
stashed it in his pocket,
blessed himself,
blessed his lunch,
blessed his wife.
blessed the day he met her.

She has been writing him a note,
every day of the week,
since she started staying home,
when their first child was born,
twenty years ago!
And with greatest delight,
the sixty year young man,
ate a home-made sandwich,
garnished with affection.

"Does your wife pack your lunch?"
He asked his friend, one day.
"She's a homemaker, too, isn't she?"

"She is a homemaker,"
the awe-struck friend answered.
"But she's a modern woman."

"We're blessed in different ways,"
Ram concluded,
and put away his lunch box.

CATHOLICS

We're Catholics.
We don't discriminate.
We believe in equality, eternally.

In one of his letters, St Paul proclaims:
There's no distinction:
Christ is all. Christ is in all.
So with B.A's, M.A's, and PhD's
one isn't better than another who is unlettered.
So stop harping on qualifications.
Disabuse the false notion
of racial discrimination.
Christian doctrine was the sole criterion.
Besides, the candidate was terminally ill,
she was promoted to fulfil God's will.

We are Catholics.
We don't discriminate.
We believe in equality, eternally.

DINING IN THE RECTORY

Being a man of common caste
he had to quickly find someone,
from whom to take the lead,
when it was time to dine.
So he focused on Father,
who crossed himself piously
and began to say grace.
The layman, by no means,
lacked general comportment,
but a seven course supper,
with deacon, priest and bishop,
in the hallowed dining hall
was rather hair-raising.

The host, the parish priest,
proposed a toast for his guests,
with wine of rare vintage,
in lead crystal glasses,
that complemented fine china,
and sparkling sterling silver,
meticulously laid out
on an ornate, oak table,
one hundred years old.
After salads and soups,
salmon was served,
and steak and lobster.
Stuffed quail followed,
and barbecued hare.
After a few glasses of wine
that was liberally served,
the lay guest had lost
all his inhibitions.
But he was too full,
didn't have room for dessert.

So he passed on all the pies,
pastries, cakes and ice cream.
and also refused the liqueurs that followed.

"Dinner was delicious, dear.
Fit for deacon priest and bishop,"
the layman later told his wife.
"But I can't eat like that often,
or I'll blow up like Father.
and bankrupt this home."

IDOLATRY

they worship stone,
they bow to statues
they pray to hordes of gods
and sell their pagan souls,
the godly man bemoaned,
clutching his plastic beads
praying devoutly
both eyes shut tight
forehead wrinkled

he invoked saints
he invoked martyrs
in their honour
he lit candles
burned incense
sprinkled holy water

he faced the cross
ornately carved
genuflected
and intently prayed
for the deliverance
of idol-worshipping,
pagans who bow to statues
and pray to hordes of gods

NOVENAS

She offered countless novenas,
to St Anthony, her patron,
who rewarded her handsomely,
the retiree affirmed.
Impressed by her devoutness,
I earnestly entreated
that she pray for me, too.
She readily acquiesced,
and took contributions
to pay for votive candles.
After a number of months,
after oodles of offerings,
for candles and novenas,
the retiree condemned me
as heathen without hope.
"That, without a doubt, is why
the saint didn't respond."
She took leave of me that day,
went straight to the front office
and demanded an audience.
She cited her credentials
as a retired Sister
asked that I be suspended
or interdicted forthwith.
Providentially for me
I was cautioned quietly
and I kept my employ.

Regrettably for Sister,
she had a severe seizure
that lasted a decade,
before she died.

PRAYERS

The faithful offer prayers
for righteous and sinners,
young old, sick, whole,
bachelors, benedicts,
widowers, widows.
They pray for all families:
extended, nuclear,
single parent, same sex.
They pray for towns and hamlets
in good times and bad,
for nations that are prosperous,
and those that are penurious.
At one time they prayed
for the consecration of Russia.
The faithful pray often
for myriads of intentions.
Despite such miscellany,
it sounded strange, one day,
when with grave urgency,
a pious practitioner
announced her intention,
to offer a prayer,
exclusively for blacks.
As I stared at her silently,
she sensed my disgust,
and added an amendment:
she'd pray only for blacks
who were deeply troubled.
As she made for the door,
I politely proposed
she say a prayer for herself,
and other white people, too.

STORM IN THE CATHEDRAL

All the fires of hell raged,
when the neophyte arrived,
and unwittingly sat down
on a pew meant for dignitary.
The deacon was summoned
to have him removed forthwith.
An usher was ordered
to have the seat cleansed.
The pastor was admonished,
to ensure protocol was followed.

Thence tags were affixed,
and barriers installed,
to shelter dignitary
from crass impropriety.

And feathers remained unruffled,
for decades at the Cathedral,
until a staunch admirer
of Martin Luther King,
questioned the status quo.
The rich cited privilege.
The poor cited gospel,
The priest suggested prayer,
so good judgement could prevail.
Thence only three pews:
the first second and third
were stringently reserved
for attending dignitary.

JOB HUNTING

at the canadian mission school
the vacancy was filled,
i applied at lutheran high,
but i did not pass latin,
so they did not employ me,
to teach chemistry and math
there were a few vacancies
at the presbyterian school
but hiring was frozen
because father was in scotland
on a two month holiday
didn't go to st mary's
i wasn't a catholic
couldn't teach hindu kids and muslims

did you try holy angels
my nanny asked gravely
your uncle anand worked there
as an interim teacher once
and he wasn't anglican
or any kind of christian
take a little offering
or a big one for father
and make an application

i have already done that
said the young lady choking
offering is not enough
she muttered dejectedly
so what else they want then
nanny was flabbergasted
the young lady was bashful
so her mother replied

aurat, aurat khoodo
(wife they looking for, wife)
Nasty barefaced
Bakra Bara Chooda!
my nanny screamed madly
he should go and ask his mother!

MS. SINGH

Good morning, how are you today?
You look funny, say, are you gay?
You are tanned, too, are you *Paki?*
Don't look like that, just answer me.
She recoiled, and frowned in disgust
as the lad stood and stared at her bust.
He then broke out into a raucous laugh;
flatulated; and faked a cough.

Was it not a legitimate question?
What was the reason for her objection?
Was it not being small-minded and petty
to consider childishness bigotry?
Besides, being so extremely sensitive
could prove upsetting and self -destructive.
He is just a high-spirited student,
naïve perhaps, but not delinquent.
And being curious about her complexion,
he asked an honest, innocuous question.

As Ms Singh listened pensively that day,
she breathed in deeply, and started to pray
to be able to discern the difference
between churlishness, and childish innocence

SHELLY BRAHM

It was Terry's last year,
and Lee Anne's last but one,
at the school,
Ms. Brahm told McPherson,
the new principal at Job's.
She was a single mom
who became a widow
almost six years ago.
She used public transit,
the site was convenient.
She had worked there for years.

I'm an objective man,
I'll let you know, Ms Brahm,
I don't make decisions
based on emotion.
I've filled the position.

With God's help I made it.
Lee Anne finished college,
Terry is a doctor.
Know what happened to him
after he retired,
the *aso* got cancer.
He has since become senile.

They've petitioned for prayers,
I heard in church yesterday.
Shelly Brahm chuckled,
then crossed herself quickly,
and prayed for forgiveness,
and prayed for McPherson.

ARMAGEDDON

On a desultory day,
one mid-summer afternoon,
I conjured all my courage,
to venture outside.
Massive clouds of aphids
enveloped my body,
penetrated my nostrils,
infiltrated my lungs,
blurred by vision,
made my eyes tear.
My exposed skin itched.
My mind went berserk.

Was this the precursor
of dreaded inferno?
Had Armageddon come?
I dashed to my car
turned on the ignition,
heard it cough and sputter,
and watched it belch smoke.
I turned on the AC,
and cranked it up full blast.

I woke up sweating.
I thanked God it was a dream.

GRENADIAN SUN

When the little mullets,
scurried willy nilly,
beneath your intrusive feet,
I could understand.
When the snowy egret
flapped its wings haughtily,
and hurriedly flew away,
I could understand.
When those prying chicken hawks,
crabbed and gawked and cawed
from their perch atop the cliff,
I could understand.
But I could never understand
why the good Grenadian sun
chose to hide behind the cloud,
after a single glimpse
of a true island daughter,
swimming in a mountain stream.

What did it take umbrage of?
Your long absence,
from the idyllic island?
Your foreign swim suit,
the scent of your body lotion,
or some such concern?

Or tell me, friend, truly,
lighten my befuddlement.
Did you, by any chance,
tempted by the seclusion,
decide to take a dip in the nude,
and made the sun run cover?

PAWN BOILER

Once or twice a year,
a pawn boiler man,
went to an island
in the Caribbean
to do seasonal work.
The man never divulged
the name of the island,
to either friend or foe.
But he told everyone,
without hesitation,
of its pristine beaches,
and exotic flora and fauna.
The cuisine he described,
was so tantalizing,
it made men's mouth water.
The island's inhabitants
were so hospitable,
friendly and kind,
he found a haven,
away from home.

"What language do they speak?"
someone eagerly queried.
"Patois, French and Spanish."
the pawn boiler replied.
"They don't speak English,
American English?"

"They speak no kind of English,
only Patois, French and Spanish."
"I am puzzled, my friend.
If they don't speak Yankee English
how did you acquire your accent?"
"Well, I travel back and forth,

on American Airlines,
two or three times a year.
and the hosts, hostesses,
pilots, co-pilots,
speak American English,"
said the pawn boiler man,
in a fine American twang.

Awakened early that evening,
by men's riotous laughter,
the angry owls hooted madly.
And one disgruntled creature,
circled above the gathering,
took careful aim, raised its tail high,
dumped on the pawn boiler's head,
tooted with glee, and vanished in the night.

Are there owls in your island, too?
someone asked the pawn boiler,
as he hurried home that night.

BIG APPLE

To ease the teeming congestion,
on the roads and underground
they were building light transit
over the Vanwyck Parkway,
from the airport to the city.

There's ample shopping everywhere,
only minutes away from home.
There are colleges for the kids,
and sprawling urban centers.
Culture's alive in Manhattan,
and the other three boroughs.
The devout worship freely,
in mosques and mandirs,
synagogues and shrines.
Facilities abound
for sick and healthy
young and old.
I'll never go down south,
and forsake the Big Apple,
the best city in the States:
the best city in the world.

"The Big Apple has big roaches,"
my young son stuttered suddenly,
lifting his feet alertly,
to avoid the crawling critters
"We take the good with the bad,"
the staid host remarked.
"Well, we'll stick with the good,"
my young son rejoined.
"Toronto the Good!"

FLAG BEARER
Pt. Chandricka Persaud

Not confined by institution,
nor constrained by curriculum,
he had the looming world as stage,
and ambition as sole director.
When he did not battle the elements,
day by day to eke out an existence,
he mingled with men of lucid minds,
men: the unsung sages of their time.
He drank from Gosai's fountain of wisdom;
He bathed in the Brahman's spring of knowledge;
He cloned his dad's undying industry,
He aped his mom's fervour for finesse.
He blossomed forth like a strange oasis,
that spreads and outstrips its barren environ.
Thus Queens, The Bronx, Manhattan, Brooklyn,
have been all graced by the good man's presence.
Like stars at night, his words illuminate
the sacred teachings of the holy books.
And the wisdom he shares from the *Vedas,*
Upanishads, Ramayana and *Gita,*
in pain or pleasure at funeral or feast
has never failed to appease,
the hearts of all his devotees.

BENJIE

He was only thirteen,
so he forged his ID.
It wasn't difficult,
for no one took notice.
And the soot that enveloped him
was perfect camouflage,
for his frail boyish frame.
Thus undisturbed,
he brandished cutlass
on sugar cane stalk,
and hoisted cane bundles
onto his childish head,
while his rickety neck
quaked, in vain, in protest.
His calloused soles
were indifferent
to ruptures gouged,
by razor sharp stubs,
as he trudged, body bowed,
to discharge his load.

To make ends meet,
when he left the fields,
he went to the seaside,
or adjacent mud flat,
with cast net or seine,
to catch fish or shrimp,
or buck crab in its season.
When the fishing was sparse,
and cane cutting was over,

he trapped game in the wild,
and foraged for fruit.
When conditions demanded,
he even boiled bush rum.
But despite his steadfastness
he was dogged by deprivation
till the day he emigrated.

In Ohio things were different.
He worked on a production line,
for eight hours, every day.
He fed himself well-
he even bought dentures
to enjoy the fare fully.
He slept on a bed,
for the first time in his life.
He wore a ring on his finger,
in fulfilment of a dream.
He acquired a town house.
He was happy he declared,
America was his haven
where he worked a little,
and afforded a lot!

Enjoy America, Benjie,
his cousin said brusquely.
Our sweat and blood leeched here
and our forefathers', too,
through an immense net work
of imperialist conduits.

Enjoy America, my friend!

DEPORTATION

Head, toes, knees, backside they scrutinized,
and nooks and crannies between his thighs.
They ex-rayed liver, bladder, lights, lungs,
probed urine, stool, saliva, semen.
Demanded substantive evidence,
that he didn't have a criminal record,
that his character was undefiled,
before he could enter the promised land,
with his wife and his two-year old son.
He was so elated he worked for joy,
day and night like other immigrants,
and took great pride in his growing fortune,
and lived in delight with his teenaged kids.
Suddenly, fate dealt a crippling blow:
His teenage son could endure no more,
and struck back to defend his dignity.
The law which was once deaf to his pleas,
swooped down on him immediately,
and directed that he be deported
to the land he'd left as a young child-
blameless, harmless, totally unsullied.
The learned judge who made the ruling
was the descendent of immigrants
who for abhorrent crimes they had contrived
were irrevocably exiled,
to the perils of a new colony,
just two generations earlier.

ENTICEMENT

A starving vulture,
in frantic search of food
spotted fresh prime flesh,
left unattended.
Enticed, it pounced,
and ate voraciously.
It made one more foray,
then another and another
and fortified itself
with little exertion.
For lack of exercise
for a prolonged period,
its wings atrophied;
its body ballooned.
The vulture was condemned
to amble on earth,
till the ignominy ended
when a predator pounced
on his top-heavy frame.

I WOULD HAVE...

Had I gotten my transfer,
I would have gone up to him,
looked him straight in the eyes,
stuck my middle finger out,
and said: "You dirty bastard…"
But he would have debased the word
the debauched cretin.

"Why don't you retire now?"
I would have asked him,
"And stop spreading your disease,
your insipid misanthropy,
which like an active tumor,
squelches the joy of living.
Why don't you go to hell, now,
lest Satan bar you later,
for fear you might displace him.
But that, to you would be a fillip.
Say, can you exact payback now
for the truth I tell, and you detest?
Will you dial the devil,
your dearest brother in deed,
in hell's head office?

How I wish I had gotten the transfer!

IT'S ONLY ME

She spanked him she claimed,
without any qualm.
It was her prerogative,
being teacher of standing,
and matriarch of the school.
Everyone applauded.

He grabbed him by the hair,
the principal claimed
without qualm.
Threw him against the wall,
because he stood firmly,
in loco parentis.
Everyone applauded.

He grabbed him by his arm,
hoisted him in the air,
carried him off bodily,
confined him all day,
till he confessed,
despite his innocence,
the superintendent claimed
without qualm.
Everyone applauded.

I censored his action
asked that lies be retracted,
and damage restored.
I was impugned
and condemned.
Everyone applauded.
But truth set me free,
while they wallow in the mud
of falsehood every day.

RADICAL

He slandered my ancestors.
He was just a child they said,
emotionally disturbed,
who was deserted by his mother
and abused by his father.
He hurled a text book at me,
I dodged, he hit his classmate.
Had I not dodged, they cautioned, sternly,
the harm to the child might have been thwarted.
I lost my wallet one day,
got pee in my coffee mug,
was called a racist name.
Forgive him they admonished,
seventy-seven times or more.
Then he swore at Ms. Higgins,
and got in real deep trouble:
a three-day suspension.
a threat of expulsion.
He sneaked behind me
while I worked at my desk,
I turned around to look,
he blew a breath at me and laughed.
spittle spattered on my face.
I was shocked, I almost gagged.
When I got up, the chair nudged him.
He hurried to the office,
they gave him a candy.
My action was censored.
I was rebuked most sternly.
and Christendom died that day.

HALLOWEEN

Halloween morning,
the vice principal
stood in the school yard,
dressed up like a witch,
with a pointed hat,
a straight broom stick,
discolored front teeth,
protruding canines,
blood shot eyes,
aquiline nose,
mule-like ears -
she was right at home
in a witch's outfit.
It gave her grace
because she smiled today,
as people passed by.
Her principal, too,
who stood at her side,
had a gargantuan smile.
The kids lauded
and applauded,
for the unclad clown,
and his vice-
the costumed witch.

EYELESS

Gruesome grimace.
Explosive spasms.
Cavernous sockets.
Eyeless.
The eyeless face
was equally expressionless,
the nemesis discerned.

He reinserted one eye,
squishy, slippery
and then the other.
He looked again intently.
Still no expression,
But the pupils rolled inwards,
and two white globes rolled out.

Once again, the nemesis
extracted the eyes.
Holding one in each hand,
he focused both
on their hapless owner,
and brusquely declared:

Accursed lecher, view now,
the grief you inflicted on others.
And then, see no more!
He stamped on the left eye.
He stamped on the right,
laughed derisively,
spat, and walked away.

COOLIE

You didn't call white colliers coolie,
You didn't call white vassals coolie
Why did you call my forebears coolie?
Why did you call their off springs coolie?
Was it for the same reason
you called black people nigger-
your pink-eyed derision
of their pristine complexion?
We don't decry your innate paleness
We don't dream to derogate you.
Follow the lead: strive to be gallant:
Don't call me coolie,
or my black comrade nigger!
Don't denigrate our unspoiled colour!

DETAILS

Size of weapon.
Caliber of munition.
Intensity of explosion.
Effect of impact.
Extent of damage.

Soldier's stats.
Eye colour.
Hair texture.
Gait, composure.
Demeanour.

Date of attack.
Time, place.
Others in squad.
Details
ad nauseam.
Ear drums explode.
Stomach curdles.
One more death!

EFFICACY

A finger, bent,
bony, wasted,
dried a tear drop
shed from sunken eye,
to wrinkled cheek.
And moved by the kindness
of a mother who won't
withdraw the raw teat
of her wilted breast,
from a hungry child's
rapacious pummeling,
I couldn't recant the lie
that made the tramp exult.
I shamelessly confirmed,
that a make-believe kin
had sent him the gift.
As I watched him,
steeped in deep delight,
caress the small package,
I myself had wrapped,
I silently extolled
the efficacy of a lie!

EPITHETS

I took umbrage one evening,
when the hostess was addressed,
as 'Old Lady,' by a guest.
I promptly informed him,
in a hushed, humble, tone
of my grave disapproval,
of the uncouth appellation.
The man remonstrated wildly:
The phrase 'Old Lady,' he upheld,
was indeed most innocuous.
But 'Old Lady' is not her name,
it's a just a crude epithet.
My friend remained adamant.
He became deeply enraged.
Forced to defend myself,
I posed him a question:
What if I call you 'Bald Head'
or 'Big Belly,' my good friend?
Would you take to it kindly?
The man's bald head became red.
His big belly bobbed wildly
He didn't say one more word.
Was he convinced that epithets
like 'Old Lady and Bald Head'
were distasteful, if not rude?

FIGHTER

I fight, my friends,
to the bitter end,
like my forebears before me.
Though there be mountains to climb,
though there be rivers to cross,
though there be chasms to traverse,
in darkness or light,
in wind, hail or sleet,
I fight, my friends,
to the most bitter end.
But like a noble warrior,
who does not fight unarmed foe,
nor hurt the sick or dying
I do not fight the imbecilic.

FAITHFUL FRIEND

I call, my friend, and you are always there,
not mindful when you call, I do not hear.

I call with the crickets and the night owl,
I call when phantoms of the mind play foul.

I call, when the cardinal calls its mate,
and you commiserate or celebrate.

I call, my friend, and you are not upset
that I was deaf, when you were cold and wet.

I call, and you promptly forgo your meal,
thus strongly of our friendship do you feel.

I call, and no deceit do you suspect
when to our joint agreement, I object.

Forever, I shall call, my faithful friend,
for head, and hand and heart and all you lend.

FRIEND

Lulled by her soft sibilating voice,
he began to carefully rationalize:
Her blue eyes bespeak the same piousness,
of a righteous nun proffering kindness…
Her acumen, her refinement
shone like stars in the firmament.
Leisure, lean cuisine, assiduities… absurd!
Amity, endearment, integrity… indeed!
The virtuous never deign to feign,
he surmised, and surrendered again.
She reached out, he was entranced,
with celestial grace they embraced and danced.

Thence, forsaken, he sat in no man's land,
Whence he watched her swoon in another man's hands.

WHY YOU?

The man was big and bald,
with bushy unkempt beard.
They did not like his looks.
They said he smelled of curry,
which he abstained from eating
because of severe allergies.

At work, every morning
they smelled booze in his breath,
though the man was abstemious,
as a Himalayan monk.

His countenance, he surmised,
gave rise to their derision,
But what with his young colleague?
She was pretty, petite,
fashionable, friendly,
intelligent, resilient
didn't speak with an accent;
didn't eat sardine sandwich.
She had an anglicized name,
how did she arouse disdain?
It must be, he presumed,
the permanent light tan,
that she never had to pay for.

WELL KEMPT

In the sixties and seventies
when fashion statements were made
with unshorn beards,
and long hair
and bell bottom pants,
a pious priest,
almost out of his elements,
poignantly decried
the all pervasive madness.
Go get groomed he charged,
so you can face God Almighty,
and be able to seek
his infinite mercy.
Though he was growing old,
the goodly priest affirmed,
he took pride in his person,
and kept himself well groomed.
Even when he went to the clinic
for bi-weekly transfusions,
he took particular care,
for the team of young nurses
were prepossessing women,
and the other personnel
were always prim and proper.

As I looked at the priest
laying well-shorn in his casket,
I stroked my grey beard,
and prayed for his soul.

THE VOW

whether in good times or bad,
before man, woman and god,
he raised up his right hand,
and swore to be her husband…
to cherish and adore her
to honour her forever.

so when he came home one day,
and caught his good wife at play,
she looked at him for a while,
and with an unabashed smile,
reminded him of his oath,
and bade him not be loathe.

then, instead of being jealous,
the man waxed magnanimous.
and the strength of the sacred vow
upheld the marriage somehow.

VENGEANCE

I got him today!
She chuckled with glee.
Big riot it was.
I wore a short dress,
without any tights.
I saw the man gag.
I thought he would die.
He was right behind me,
when I let go freely,
and felt fully vindicated,
after waiting several years.
But I paid a price too.
I gasped and I gagged
I nearly dropped dead.
I had to weather the storm,
I did not dare to waver,
for my goodly superior,
despite doing it for years,
would have fired me promptly,
if he had the slightest proof,
I was the perpetrator,
because my blow was more potent
than all his combined efforts,
over several long years.
Though he came in next morning
with a gas mask as armour,
he didn't take another chance
he instantly transferred me
to a distant station.

UNCLE LAMB / DAVY ROSE

Governor General Davy Rose died.
Tons of scaffolding fell on his head.
He was visiting royalty in England.
With due protocol his embalmed corpse,
was promptly flown back to his homeland.
And for two full weeks, torrents of tributes
inundated the local air waves.

Uncle Lamb died of asphyxiation,
when he was pinned under his Ferguson
that turned turtle in the muddy back dam.
They brought him out on a jute bag stretcher
dressed him in his khaki outfit,
placed him in a box board coffin,
carried him on a farm trailer,
buried him the next day,
in an untended cemetery
and left him in a world of silence,
while the country's airwaves
still paid copious tribute
to Davy Rose, governor general,
for whom a mausoleum was built,
while his body laid in state,
in an flag-draped, oak casket.

Don't give a damn an old man declared.
My friend wuk and wuk till he drop' dead,
an' we bury him quick,
in a box board coffin.
He mus' be rotting by now.
And wha' de govern'r man Rose really do?
Did he wuk and wuk, like my buddy Lamb did?
What wuk did govern'r man do,
to deserve so much *adelation*?

O'SHEA'S TV

Mr. Thomas O'Shea,
was so flummoxed one day,
he turned red from head to toe,
like an over ripe tomato.
For, to his grave consternation,
he learnt that his friend's television,
was a very early model
that couldn't be hooked up to cable.
Christ, it's hard to perceive,
the type of life you live,
without such basic amenity,
in the twentieth century.
Say, in the country you come from,
did you have a TV in your home?
Indeed I did, I tell no lie,
the other man replied,
but I hardly ever watched TV,
for fear my brain would atrophy.
Well you must lead a boring life,
like my goodly Guyanese wife,
who nags me almost constantly,
and even unplugs the darned TV,
so I could go with her for a walk,
or so we'd just sit and talk
about Plato, Kant, Rene Descartes,
Spinoza, Hume or Jean Paul Sartre.
But I don't care a mite for philosophy,
I prefer watching my programs on TV.

SPITTING MAESTROS

The batter comes to the plate.
He spits.
The pitcher steps on the mound.
He spits.
He pitches.
He spits.
The batter swings.
Strike three.
He spits.
Ball four.
He spits.
The batter walks.
He spits.
The pitcher balks.
He spits.
Fair ball.
He spits.
Fly ball.
He spits.
Ground ball.
He spits.
Home run.
He spits.
Diving stop.
He spits.
Running catch.
He spits.
The infielder spits.
The outfielder spits.
The short stop spits.
The catcher spits.
The coach spits.
The umpire spits.
They all spit!
like Canada geese,
that lift their tails and shit.

PICKLED PESTLE

He was given free boarding.
He was given free lodging.
He was granted assiduities
and abundant human kindness.

And having received, he reciprocated.
He gave subtle hints whenever he could,
on the scope for more magnanimity,
and deeper respect for Christian doctrine.

He also paid compliments to my spouse.
And one fateful day, while I was away,
He tried to comfort his lonesome hostess.
"Accept my kindness, now," the good guest urged.
"For you, my dear, have always been so kind."

"Such heartfelt warmth!" the hostess replied,
as she seized and severed with a single swipe,
the spirited, upright, rod of kindness,
the gracious guest generously proffered.

"Accept my gift, now," the hostess exhorted
as she gave the lodger a clear glass jar,
with a pickled pestle floating inside.

MY NORTH / SOUTH FRIEND

Are you on the South side or North? he asked
It depends, she said after a brief pause.

Depends on what? Her good friend enquired.
It depends on the direction you're coming from.
He'd leave soon he said coming from the east.
Would be going directly westbound from east?
Directly westbound, he said, and he wasn't too far.

Will you be driving or taking the bus?
He would drive he said and should arrive soon.
In the afternoon, dear, or evening? she asked
At six p. m. sharp he swiftly replied.
I do wish to see you, please don't be late.

Are you on the South side or North? he asked
It depends, she said after a brief pause.

It depends on if you're coming east or west.
Coming west, you would find me on the North.
Coming east you would find me North *of* South.
If you don't find the place, do give me a call.
I have to go, someone's knocking on my door.
Bye, North/South friend.
Enjoy your visitor!

MEN PLAY FOR MILLIONS

Expertly,
like cockatiel,
men split seed,
champ,
spit tons of shell.

Like ruminants
men chew gum,
or select tobacco.
And like Canada geese,
that lift their tail,
and defecate at will,
men artfully spit
on the slick green turf,
in swanky stadiums,
where they play ball,
for millions of dollars

If the geese were rewarded,
like the million dollar men,
for their precise artistry,
would they, one day become
million dollar geese
and infest the earth
with filth?

LIVING ROOM CLOCK

On Halloween, it stopped at 12 mid-night.
I changed the batteries on All Saints morning,
but none of the hands of the old clock budged.
The clock didn't work until Christmas Eve,
but on Christmas morning, when I awoke,
to my great surprise it started ticking.
And I noted that the time was correct.
A few weeks later the clock began to lag,
by minutes at first, by hours later.
I promptly replaced the two old batteries,
but none of the hands of the old clock budged,
until the morning of Easter Monday.
It worked well until the summer solstice,
then stopped again, and didn't work for months.
I got mad one day and stuck masking tape,
on the face of Judas Iscariot,
wary not to offend the others,
who were partaking of the last supper.
When that did not help, I bought a new clock,
one that chimed on top of the hour.
And from the time I hung the new clock up,
my good old clock started ticking again.
And from that very day, for years on end,
the clock without fail kept time exactly.
For good measure, I left the masking tape
on Judas Iscariot's bearded face.

HI DAD

In the last six months, things have changed
dreadfully drastically, Dad.
Though the plot of land you planted
throve and yielded bountifully,
almost everything else went haywire.
One day Uncle Merlin came by.
Mom was chasing the neighbour's cows
that were grazing in the garden.
The old lecher made a pass at me.
I thought I would die of shame and shock.
I told him, I'd tell his daughter,
Sandra, who is sixteen like me.
Shire used to keep watch for us,
but thieves still stripped the combine bare.
We couldn't replace the stolen parts,
so we couldn't sell the machine,
in order to pay down the loan.
And the bank threatened to foreclose.
My mom has not got back the gun
she had surrendered when you were gone,
so she can't fire in the air,
to frighten the thieves
when they raid the poultry farm.
I'm worried, mom hardly sleeps now.
People rarely stop by these days,
Your old friends have disappeared
with all the money they owed.
It's been really hard, since you left.
It feels so strange without you here,
It feels stranger writing to you,
knowing my letter can't be mailed.
But it feels so good to write, Dad.
I'll write again another day.
Maybe, next time,
I'll have good news to share.
Love you,
Goodbye.

FLIP SIDE

I woke up at six,
sat on a recliner
beside the gas fire place,
sipped fresh coffee
and read the morning paper.
I shaved and showered,
had a hearty breakfast,
before driving off to work
that started at nine.
When I returned home at five,
and saw my son's twisted ankle,
I patted his head,
and gently consoled him.

"Shut up. Stop complaining!"
my father had admonished,
when in my childhood
I had twisted my ankle.
It was long past sunset
when he had returned home,
hungry, thirsty, grimy
totally fatigued
and too tired to empathize.
What great dissimilarity
between plenitude and poverty!

Both fathers loved their sons.

WESTERNIZING

My Canadian girlfriend, Kaitlin,
wanted to westernize me.
She couldn't change my complexion,
or height or hair colour,
so she decided to work on my accent.
Vogaay, she insisted gravely,
Vogaay, not Vaughan,
Vogaay… Dr Vogaay.

Good morning, *Dr Vogaay,*
I greeted most cordially.
Dr Vaughan, he corrected,
I listened incredulously.
After being drilled for weeks,
to say *Dr Vogaay.*
my tongue knotted up,
when I tried Dr Vaughan.
The interview ended early.
Kaitlin took me to task,
for being too hifalutin,
and almost laughed her head off,
when I used the word albumen.
Egg white, we say in Canada,
she half-laughed, half- chastised.
You say potato; not potahto,
so it's tomato not tomahto
I listened to Kaitlin,
perforce day by day,
till at last she decided
to tackle my name:
Kesh sounds too Indian.
Quiche, as in quiche lorraine
is more Western,
she propounded.

Indeed, I agreed.
But you know what,
You could take your quiche,
your lorraine,
your Canadian
and your Western,
and stuff them up your Southern.
Never saw her again.

SPINSTER TALK

I have to find a man
who is tall, muscular,
graceful and good-looking,
with a taste for French cuisine,
a flair for fine fashion,
a good sense of humor,
and love of adventure…

I have to find someone,
the perfect gentleman,
who'll serve breakfast in bed,
pack my lunch on work days,
cook supper every night,
do my laundry and his,
take the dog out for walks…

Next time, said Donna,
who had been divorced twice,
I'll have to find someone
who's really compliant,
so I can train him well,
from the very first day,
so he'd not make mistakes.

First time I make a hit,
I'll have to get it right,
Adrienne affirmed,
with a broad wrinkled smile.

So do I, added Grace,
staring at the distance.
and proposed one more toast,
for the fifty-fifth birthday.
of the sprightly spinster, Moll.

BIG LAUGH

The steam sizzled and scalded her hand.
It dripped on her feet, she started and stomped.
Her eyes welled up, she checked the tear.
She snubbed her pain and started to laugh

She slapped her spouse across the face,
spat on her stepson who complained,
raved and ranted at her in-laws,
then she cooled down and started to laugh.

An irate client swore at her.
A close co-worker slandered her.
Her old boss tried to wheedle her.
She stayed unfazed and started to laugh.

A cop stopped her on the highway,
looked at her licence, checked his records
and declared the licensee dead.
She said O.K. and started to laugh.

She locked herself out of the car,
And heard torrents of torrid taunts,
then her blind date did not show up.
But she stayed serene; she started to laugh

Once she went to see her physician
Who said her tumour was so malignant,
that within a few months she would die.
She listened calmly and started to laugh.

And she laughed and laughed again and again,
And lived for many more months and years.
Laughing and laughing all her woes away!

MAN DOWNSTAIRS

I incanted mantras,
invoked the Muses
prayed to St Jude.
In utter desperation
I called on my friend
a poet of standing.
He wrote:
The man downstairs
is elegant and tall
like a Nubian prince.
His sleek dark skin
glows like fine ebony.
His cultured smile
sets in me a swoon-
bewilders me totally-
my head whirls
and legs wobble,
my body quakes.

As the man downstairs approaches,
his mass of muscles,
rippling like a rustic lake fanned
by a soft Kilimanjaro breeze
I stare in rapt enthrallment,
and long to feel those muscular limbs
wrapped around me forever.
My heart flutters like humming birds' wings.
I explode with excitement
and I thank God I'm able to dream, at least:
that one day,
the man downstairs
would walk upstairs,
and sweep me off my two feet.

When my friend heard this part,
his mind went berserk-
He began to fantasize,
like only a poet could,
that he was the Nubian prince.
I swiftly kicked him,
in his desire
and he howled like a dog,
and came back to reality.

MAPLE LEAF
(For Marlene)

Like an eagle flying in the sky,
She flutters freely way up high.
Heralding hope!
Pronouncing peace!
Proclaiming freedom!
Professing justice!
A song of love in the wind she sings,
Announcing warm and cheerful greetings
From snow-capped peaks of lofty mountains,
From lush, luxuriant, rolling, plains.
From east to west, from sea to sea,
From north to south where're you may be
Her flaming red, her snowy white
Indeed present a wondrous sight.
Oh most magnificent Maple Leaf!
To countless hearts you bring relief!

ROAD DONKEY

I steered to the right,
the donkey went right.
I steered to the left,
the donkey went left.
Stupid donkey!
The goat got away,
and the sheep and the horse.
The cows bellowed a bit,
but they budged at last.
And so did the dog and the duck,
and the fowl and the hog.
I honked hard on my horn,
the donkey turned around,
stared me in the face,
stood on his hind legs
and started to bray.
I pelted him with an orange.
He became enraged.
He backed up madly,
lifted his tail high,
and defecated at will,
on the hood of the car.
The donkey still reigns,
I noted resignedly.

ROAD RAGE

High beams flashed,
Horns blasted.
Fists clenched.
Teeth gritted.
Middle finger.
Bulging eyes.
Twitching nose.
Contorted face.
Windows rolled down.
Heads popped out.
Imprecations.
Accusation.
Mothers abused.
Culture inculpated.
Race incriminated.
Rage ignited.
Violence threatened.
Gun pulled.
Hammer cocked.
Blood
Sirens
Mangled flesh.
Fire trucks.
Splintered bones
Ambulance.
Corpse
Police.
Road rage.

THE MONEYED MAN

Guess who I saw at the ten o'clock mass,
Who? asked his mom, growing rather curious.
Take a guess mom, insisted her young son,
as she flipped the strips of sizzling bacon.
Was it Brendan and his twin brother Bill?
Wrong again mom, one more try, chuckled Phil.
Must be Mr. Thom, your home room teacher.
or Mrs. Curry, from the school choir.
Phil took some bacon and started to munch,
as he helped his mom with their Sunday brunch.

The question arose again as they ate,
Phil's dad joined in, he didn't hesitate.
Will you tell us Phil who really it was
you saw today, at the ten o'clock mass?

I saw him too, put in Phil's friend Matthew,
way at the back in the very last pew.
Some people looked back and stared at his face,
as if he had just come from outer space.
I don't think they should have stared the man down,
Matthew continued with an impish frown.

For the man was not a guilty offender
just because he was a well-moneyed lawyer.

THE STRONGEST SURVIVE

Joshua Kumar (guest poet)

Inspired by the bloody cross
They slaughtered the dissenters
Spread their lies among the masses
Claimed Christ as their mentor

Christ-God sat silent as it happened
Watched innocents die
Let them profane his holy name
With cruel deceit and lies

The death toll rose
The Christians found
No shortage of
Enemies to kill

They rationalized
The blood on their hands thus:
They were instruments of god's will

Their leaders,
The infallible popes
Were god's elite
On earth

Only they could
Divine the Divine Will
They were blessed with
This gift at birth

They declared open season
For good, godly reason
On pagans, heretics and Jews

Through death and destruction
They established their religion
The plague they call 'good news'

Assimilation and extermination
Enabled Christianity to thrive
A reluctant testament to Darwinist truth:
Only the strongest survive

BRIEF OVERVIEW

Twiddling Thumbs

Health and Wellness. Culture and Heritage. Family Matters. Social Justice…

Within this eclectic collection of life experiences and quandaries, lie parcels of original popup nuggets filled with palatable, inspirational, heartfelt truths, weaved with skill and awesome hilarity. *Twiddling Thumbs* stimulates critical thinking while presenting opportunities for reflection and new perspectives on challenges and setbacks. This publication will inspire the Ubuntu Community Village writers, the TAIBU community at large, and readers everywhere.

Tony Jno Baptiste, Writer/Poet. Program Manager TAIBU Community Health Centre.